Where you from?

A book celebrating Black British History for Children

By SJ Penni

Illustrated by
Julian D Penni

To my wonderful children: Jack, Will and Maddie

"It's never been more important to celebrate the pioneering contributions that black women and men have made to history. Black History Month gives us the opportunity to do that. This book will be a valuable resource to help us acknowledge these inspirational stories all year round."

Foluke Akinlose MBE FRSA

"This is an important book, to help us remember and celebrate contributions from black history and to recognise that black history is also all of our history."

Margaret Casely-Hayford- first black female partner in a city law firm

"Black history is an important story to tell. History cannot exist without the truth and to tell the truth it needs to be inclusive. It's the full picture; the richness we deserve. It gives us pride, a sense of belonging, contribution and empowerment."

Elaine Banton

"A fantastic book that makes essential reading for all schoolchildren."

The Secret Barrister

"A magnificent book for all school age children. They will love it!"

Maxine Peake

Where Are You From?
A book celebrating black British history for children

By SJ Penni

Illustrated by Julian D Penni

Designed by Fountain Creative

First published in 2021 by SJ Penni

ISBN: 978-1-8380848-3-7

TAUK Kids Children's Book Publishers
A Division of Team Author UK

Picture credits

Pages 2-3: All images, Shutterstock.com; **Page 4:** Rosa Parks, Harlin Design / Shutterstock.com; John Blanke, Public domain via Wikipedia Commons; Picture frame, Shutterstock.com; Protestet, Shutterstock.com; **Page 5:** Racing car, Shutterstock.com; Notting Hill Carnival, Bikeworldtravel / Shutterstock.com; Barrister, Shutterstock.com; **Pages 6-7:** All images, Shutterstock.com; **Page 8:** West Indian soldiers, Ernest Brooks Public Domain via Wikimedia Commons; bus, Shutterstock.com; **Page 9:** Notting Hill Carnival, Vibrant Pictures / Shutterstock.com, 'Beachy Head Woman', Used with the permission of Twinkl Ltd. (c) All Rights Reserved. Visit www.twinkl.co.uk; **Page 10:** Ivory bangle lady and miner, Shutterstock.com; Benin raid objects, Public domain via Wikipedia Commons; **Page 11:** Toussaint L'Ouverture, Shutterstock.com; Barbara Beese, The National Archives UK, No restrictions, via Wikimedia Commons; **Pages 12-25:** All images, Shutterstock.com; **Page 26:** Doctor's case, Shutterstock.com; Mary Seacole etching, Public Domain via Wikipedia Commons; **Page 27:** Jacket, Shutterstock.com; Chartist riot, Alfred Pearse (1855–1933), Public domain, via Wikimedia Commons; **Pages 28-31:** All images, Shutterstock.com; **Page 32:** Sugar plantation, Shutterstock.com; The Cosways and Ottobah Cugoano, Richard Cosway, Public domain, via Wikimedia Commons; Book title page, Unknown author, Public domain, via Wikimedia Commons; **Page 33-38:** All images, Shutterstock.com; **Page 39:** Man waving and pianist, Shutterstock.com; Othello scene, Public Domain via Wikipedia Commons; **Page 40:** Marcus Rashford, Dummydum / Shutterstock.com; Lunches, Shutterstock.com; **Page 41:** Football 2020, Shutterstock.com; Rashford mural, Jon Fitton / Shutterstock.com; **Page 42:** Nelson Mandela, kirkchai benjarusameeros / Shutterstock.com; Bus, Shutterstock.com; **Page 43:** Rosa Parks statue, EQRoy / Shutterstock.com; Martin Luther King, Vectroyer / Shutterstock.com; **Page 44:** Flapper girl and baby objects, Shutterstock.com; Harriet Tubman statue, stockelements / Shutterstock.com; Harriet Tubman illustration, Harlin Design / Shutterstock.com; **Page 45:** US flag and The White House, Shutterstock.com; Harris and Biden, Illustrasi Senja / Shutterstock.com; Harris waving, TeddyandMia / Shutterstock.com; **Page 46-48:** All images, Shutterstock.com

Contents

Introduction

Each year in October we celebrate Black History Month. But who are these people, and who are the hidden figures we don't know about? Have you wondered where everyone in the country is from?

Most of us have heard of Nelson Mandela, Martin Luther King, Rosa Parks, and Malcolm X. Perhaps you have studied them in school when discussing discrimination?

In Britain, you may be familiar with sports stars such as Tessa Sanderson, Dame Kelly Holmes, boxer Nicola Adams, and Marcus Rashford, the footballer.

But what about historical figures who were British?

In this book, we are going to celebrate the lesser known figures that played a significant part in history, as well as some who are blazing a trail in the present. Prepare for a fantastically amazing journey as you meet Princess Sarah Bonetta, Paul Stephenson, Kamala Harris, Mary Seacole ... and many more!

The men and women in this book didn't set out to be thought of as great. They achieved extraordinary things simply by following their hearts, talents and dreams. They didn't listen when people said they couldn't do something. They dared to be different.

They made a difference.

I hope at the end you will see black history is, in fact, all our history. From black Tudors and black soldiers, to black princesses and professors in Britain.

Through a mix of **'Did You Know'** sections and factual showcases, this book is written to dip in and out of. I hope you can see how black history fits into all aspects of the history we are taught at school.

Whether in sport, in art, in politics, in discrimination and civil rights, black history is everywhere! I am not a historian. I am a practicing lawyer. I do, however, love history and learning about where laws came from. I hope you enjoy learning about black history too.

Sally Penni MBE

Did you know?

There are laws that affect black history in the UK. They are:

Abolition of Slavery Act (1833 and 1984)
Race Relations Act (1965)
Sex Discrimination Act (1975 and 1984)
Equality Act (2010)
Modern Slavery Act (2015)
Protection of Harassment Act (1997)

Racially aggravated offences are criminal offences. You will receive a worse sentence for your crime if it was based on someone's race.

What is Black History Month?

Black History Month, which is every October, is a chance to highlight the achievements and contributions of black people through the ages, as well as the struggles and barriers they still face in their daily lives.

Black History Month highlights historical episodes and figures not otherwise taught in UK schools. In this book, I would like to highlight just some of these. Black people have long been part of British history before Windrush and even slavery, from black Romans and Tudors to a black princess adopted by Queen Victoria and Prince Albert.

The following is a transcription of a video message given by PM Boris Johnson in October 2020. It summarises what we have always known – that black history is all our history. (You can view the full speech here: **https://t.co/7jlrsAzwY1**).

"For countless generations, people of African and Caribbean descent have been shaping our nation's story, making a huge difference to our national and cultural life and helping to make Britain a better place to be. It is this contribution of black British people that I am proud to be celebrating.

That contribution is overwhelmingly apparent today in the energy, talent and dedication of business leaders, lawyers, academics, musicians, artists, and many more. This year, we have seen the heroic efforts of all frontline workers and the doctors, nurses and medical professionals who have been tirelessly supporting our NHS throughout the coronavirus pandemic.

Of course, there is much more work to be done to ensure that every person of every skin colour, background and creed has the opportunity to succeed, and to stamp out discrimination and racism. I understand the force and depth of feeling that has been expressed following the death of George Floyd in the United States, and share the determination of all those seeking a more equal and just world. That's why I have set up a Commission on Race and Ethnic Disparities to make the progress so many have called for, and to bring about lasting change.

But I also believe that alongside tackling the substance of the problem, we should be giving due praise and recognition to all those who have played such an important role in helping to positively shape modern Britain and our modern Commonwealth.

It's a great shame that more people do not know more about Paul Stephenson or Mary Prince. Or that they haven't heard about the many brave black servicemen who served in the World Wars – from those grappling in the mud of the Western Front, to the valiant Caribbean pilots and aircrew in the Second World War, and the heroes who fought further afield, in places such as Burma. Or even that they know so little about the Windrush generation, from the nurses who were there at the very start of our NHS to all those who helped rebuild our country after the war.

A key part of the commission's work will be to look at how we ensure society is more aware of the significant role people from different ethnic backgrounds have played in our shared British history. Let's use this Black History Month to celebrate not just the achievements of people today, but of all those who have shaped our nation. Let's raise up those names. Let's remember their acts. And let's celebrate them – because black British history is all our history."

However, with black and minorities still asked 'where are you from' frequently, I wondered if it would be interesting to celebrate some of the everyday history we don't always learn at school.

Now, I cannot include all of them in this book, but I hope you will see from reading it that it features interesting people from all our history. I am not a historian but I am a girly swot. My day job is a barrister at law. I appear in courts. I use old laws written largely by dead, white men. Orchestras play music written by dead, white men.

But what about the black classicists that came before the Kanneh-Masons family who played at Prince Harry's wedding?

What about the slaves who built the theatres and statues in the UK?

Black History Overview

In all aspects of history, black people were present and made a contribution, from the music halls and concert halls built by slaves, to the rebuilding of Britain and the creation of the NHS following World War II. Here is a brief overview of some significant events in black history:

Historial Period	Approximate years	Significant Event
Roman Britain	27BC-476 AD	• Black Roman body discovered which means there were black Romans in York • Roman Africans guarded Hadrian's Wall in the North-East of England
Tudors	1485-1603	John Blanke a royal trumpeter to Henry VIII
Early Georgians	1714-1776	Paintings of well-dressed children
Victorians	1837-1901	Queen Victoria adopted Sarah Forbes Bonetta
Industrial revolution	1760-1840	Mill workers in Rochdale protested against slaves used in cotton trade which led to a cotton famine
World War I	1914-1918	Black troops recruited to fight the war. Gurkhas, black African and Indian troops all fought.
Early 20th Century	1919	Liverpool race riots
World War II	1939-1945	Black American soldiers fighting in the war
Windrush	1948	HMS Windrush brings Caribbean people to the UK to help rebuild after the war

10 Moments of British Black History

Soldiers of the British West Indies Regiment, September 1916.

1 West Indian soldiers in World War 1

15,204 men served in the British West Indies Regiment, from the Bahamas to British Guiana, however, they have largely been forgotten in Remembrance commemorations.

The soldiers faced racism from their comrades and enemies and weren't allowed to fight alongside white soldiers. Nevertheless, they carried out dangerous jobs such as loading ammunition, digging trenches, and laying telephone wires.

After moving to Italy following armistice, the soldiers mutinied, no longer willing to suffer the humiliation of cleaning clothes and latrines for white soldiers who themselves received pay rises. One soldier was executed, others imprisoned, and they were all excluded from the victory parades marking the end of the war.

2 The Bristol bus boycott

In 1963, after 18-year-old Guy Bailey was turned away from a job interview at the state-owned Bristol Omnibus Company because he was black (which was legal at the time), members of the black community, organised by Paul Stephenson, Roy Hackett and Bailey, led a boycott of the buses in protest. After four months, the bus company relented, overturning the ban on ethnic minorities working on Bristol's buses. This marked a significant step towards the UK's first laws against racial discrimination, resulting in the Race Relations Act 1965, now part of the Equality Act 2010.

3 The Notting Hill Carnival in London

Notting Hill Carnival in London is the largest street party in Europe. It began when human rights activist Claudia Jones, herself deported from the US for being a member of the Communist party and granted asylum in the UK, threw herself into anti-racist activism.

In response to the Notting Hill riots of 1958 and the racist murder of Kelso Cochrane, Jones launched an indoor Caribbean carnival in St Pancras in 1959 with the intention of bringing people together. Further indoor events were held throughout the 1960s, finally taking to the streets of Notting Hill in 1965. Notting Hill Carnival is now second only in size to Brazil's Rio carnival.

4 John Blanke, the black trumpeter

The Tudor period was significant for black settlement in Britain, although seldom mentioned in schools. John Blanke, a regular musician at the courts of both King Henry VII and Henry VIII, was one such settler. He is the first known black Briton for whom we have both their name and picture. A 60ft-long scroll commissioned by Henry VIII depicting the extravagant Westminster Tournament of 1511 shows John riding on horseback in the royal procession.

John was paid 8d* a day in wages. This doubled to 16d after he successfully petitioned the king for a pay rise.

Did you know?

Up to 300 Africans lived in Britain in the Tudor Period. A lot of them were merchants, aristocrats or belonged to royal entourages.

**d. was 'pennies' in old British money*

5 'Beachy Head woman'

A mysterious, ancient skeleton of the "Beachy Head woman", believed to be the first known person in Britain from sub-Saharan Africa, was uncovered in a village in East Sussex. She is thought to have lived nearly 1,800 years ago in 245AD, the middle of the Roman period in Britain.

6 'Ivory bangle lady'

The "ivory bangle lady", a middle-class woman of black African ancestry and one of the wealthiest inhabitants of fourth century Roman York, was discovered in 1901 inside a stone sarcophagus. She was surrounded by jewellery made of Yorkshire jet and African elephant ivory, a glass mirror and a blue glass jug. Her discovery challenged assumptions that Africans in Britain at the time were poor or slaves.

7 The sacking of Benin

Benin City was one of the oldest states in west Africa, dating back to the 11th century. In 1897, during the "Benin expedition", British troops punitively sacked the ancient city after it imposed customs duties which defied the British empire. The city's walls – four times the length of the Great Wall of China – were razed. The city was burned to the ground and its treasures were looted.

Much of Benin's stolen artworks and artefacts were taken to Britain, auctioned or gifted to museums across Europe. Hundreds of these artefacts still reside in museums across the UK. The Benin bronzes remain the subject of demands for repatriation.

Looted objects from the Benin raid

8 Britain's black miners

In the aftermath of the Second World War, amid severe labour shortages in the mining industry, black workers were invited to Britain by the government to fill vacancies in vital industries, including coalmines.

Hundreds of African-Caribbean men are estimated to have worked in the mines in Nottinghamshire, Leicestershire, Yorkshire, Bristol, Kent, Durham, South Wales and Scotland. At least a quarter of the workforce at Gedling Colliery in Nottingham, known as "The Pit of Nations", were black.

9 The Haitian Revolution

The Haitian Revolution was one of the largest slave rebellions in history, ending slavery in France's most profitable colony. The slave population of Saint-Domingue in the 18th century outnumbered the white population by 10 to one. In 1791, the enslaved began a rebellion against white landowners, led by Haitian-born Toussaint L'Ouverture, a former slave. Haiti became the first independent black republic in the Americas in 1804.

Toussaint L'Ouverture

10 The British Black Panthers

In 1968, the BBP was founded by Obi Egbuna in Notting Hill, London, inspired by the American Black Panther movement. Under Altheia Jones-LeCointe's leadership from 1970, it transformed into a highly effective organisation rooted in working-class solidarity and community activism. The Panthers focused on fighting racial discrimination in jobs, education, health, and housing.

During a protest against police brutality, nine black leaders (known as the Mangrove Nine), were arrested and charged with inciting a riot. After representing themselves and demanding an all-black jury, they were acquitted. Evidence of racial hatred in the London police was publicly acknowledged by the judge.

The arrest of Barbara Beese, a member of the Black Panthers and one of the original Mangrove Nine.

Ready to meet 31 black figures who have played a significant part in British history and are shaping our modern world? Let's begin...

Paul Stephenson

Activist and Campaigner

The moment that Paul Stephenson sat down in a pub that banned black people in 1964 was the moment he helped change Britain's discrimination laws.

When Paul walked into the Bay Horse pub in Bristol and ordered half a pint, the pub's manager told him to get out, saying: "We don't want you black people in here – you are a nuisance." Stephenson refused. He was arrested and detained in a police cell until midnight.

In 1964, banning black and Asian people from pubs and working men's clubs, and even housing and jobs, was legal in the UK. At the time that Stephenson performed his 'sit-in' at the pub in protest, he had already led a successful boycott of the city's bus company.

Following the pub sit-in, Stephenson was put on trial, which made national headlines. Eight officers, each with different versions of events, claimed that he was "aggressive" and had tried to "force his way back into the pub" which was later found to be untrue. Harold Wilson, Prime Minister at the time, sent Stephenson a personal telegram to say he would change the law. And so, in 1965, the first Race Relations Act was formed to outlaw discrimination.

Stephenson became the first black man to be made Freeman of the city of Bristol.

Growing up

Paul Stephenson was born in Rochford, Essex, in 1937. Aged three, he was evacuated to a care home in Great Dunmow, Essex, with seven white children, living there for seven years. He spent his time playing in the fields and paddling in streams, and made lifelong friends.

Stephenson felt like an outsider when he returned to London in 1947, with shouts of "blackie", "monkey" and the N-word on his walk to school. From 1948, when immigration from the colonies increased, so did the racism. While at secondary school, and being the only black child in his class, Stephenson was no longer cute and a "curiosity" like in his childhood but instead seen as a racial threat. While being caned, a teacher asked him: "Why are you looking so black?"

Stephenson joined the RAF as a cadet in 1953 and served until 1960. After the RAF, he went to college to study youth work, then moved to Bristol to become a youth and community development worker and supply teacher. Then came the bus boycott.

As the spokesman for the protesters, Stephenson won an important legal battle. However, not everyone agreed with his stance. Bill Smith, of the city's West Indian Association, believed that the protest undermined racial harmony in the city, with the Bishop of Bristol also in agreement. Those who did stand on the side of equality paid a high price. Learie Constantine, a cricketing star turned Trinidad's high commissioner, was removed from his post by the Trinidadian prime minister for his involvement.

Stephenson's activism garnered international attention. In 1964 he was invited to the US by the National Association for the Advancement of Coloured People (NAACP).

He travelled to New York City, where he met Louis Farrakhan AKA Louis X, and then went on to Richmond, in the US's segregated south, where he was met with hostility at his all-white hotel. Unbeknown to Stephenson, the NAACP had secured an agreement to desegregate the hotel and he was their test case – the first black man to stay at the John Marshall Hotel.

In 1974, Stephenson met Muhammad Ali in a hotel lobby, addressing him as Ali when many people still called him Cassius Clay, and asked him to visit his Brixton school. Ali agreed. Ali and Stephenson became friends and set up the Muhammad Ali Sports Development Association (MASDA) to give inner-city youth access to sport. In 1982, MASDA launched the British Standing Conference Against Apartheid Sports with the support of the World Boxing Association (WBA) champion

Lloyd Honeyghan.

In 1992, Stephenson returned to Bristol with his wife. He fostered eight children and campaigned for the city to acknowledge its links with slavery. In 2008, Stephenson became the first black man to be made Freeman of the city. Because of Paul Stephenson, we now have laws that protect all people from discrimination.

Sarah Forbes Bonetta

The Black Princess

Queen Victoria and her husband Prince Albert had nine children. But did you know that they also adopted a tenth child?

In 1848, orphan Sarah Forbes Bonetta was captured by the merciless King of Dahomey. She was only five years old. Before she too could be killed, Sarah was rescued by British naval officer Frederick who persuaded Sarah's captors to present the child as a 'gift' to Victoria.

Sarah Forbes Bonetta

Frederick and Sarah sailed back to England on his ship, HMS Bonetta, which became her adopted name.

Princess Sarah Forbes Bonetta grew up with Queen Victoria's children around her and was treated like a member of the queen's biological family.

The young princess married wealthy businessman Captain James Davies in 1862 and died of tuberculosis in 1880 at the age of 37.

Queen Victoria

John Kent

Britain's First Black Policeman

John Kent was born in Cumbria in 1805, beginning his duties as a police officer in Maryport in 1835 before joining Carlisle Police in 1837. John was the son of Thomas Kent, a slave who was brought into Whitehaven and freed in the UK.

It was previously thought that the first black police officer joined the Metropolitan Police in the 1960s. However, research found that John Kent served as an officer more than 100 years earlier.

A blue plaque was unveiled to commemorate John. Ian Bulman, a descendent of John who works on a dairy farm in Carlisle, said he was *"pleased and proud"*, adding that he had a *"lot of admiration of what John and his father went through."*

What are BLUE PLAQUES?

Blue plaques commemorate the link between a location and an individual who was regarded as *"eminent"* in their field.

Norwell Lionel Roberts QPM was the first black police officer to join London's Metropolitan Police, rising to the rank of Detective Sergeant. He was awarded the Queen's Police Medal in 1996.

Find out!

How many blue plaques are there in London?

Lewis Hamilton

Formula One Racing Driver

Sir Lewis Hamilton MBE was born in Stevenage in 1985. Aged five, Hamilton's dad bought him a radio-controlled car which began his fascination with racing.

The following year, Hamilton placed second against adults in the British Radio Car Association (BRCA). Aged six, his father bought him a go-kart for Christmas and promised to support his racing career as long as he worked hard at school.

Hamilton began karting in 1993 and quickly began winning races and cadet class championships. At the age of ten, he became the youngest driver to win the British cadet karting championship, and was signed to the McLaren young driver programme in 1998.

Hamilton has since won seven world titles and has overtaken Michael Schumacher's record of 91 wins in Formula One.

Having experienced bullying and racism as a child, Lewis now uses his platform to raise awareness of issues in sport, and aims to leave a legacy for a sport that lacks representation. He is a major contributor to Great Ormond Street Hospital, Unicef, The Honeypot Children's Charity and Children of Africa. He has also set up the Lewis Hamilton Foundation to provide grants and donations to help with disabilities, education and training, the advancement of health, and prevention or relief of poverty.

Formula One car

Diane Abbott

First Black Woman MP in England

Cambridge University

Diane Abbott is a British politician who has been a Member of Parliament for Hackney North and Stoke Newington since 1987.

Her school openly opposed to her applying to Cambridge University. Nevertheless, Diane Abbott fought racism – and her own party – to become Britain's first black female MP. She was called an 'extremist' by opponents and treated as a liability by Labour.

Despite having endured much criticism and abuse in recent years, Diane Abbott has been a true voice and advocate for change.

Did you know?

The first non-white Members of Parliament were elected in 1987 for the Labour Party.

The Houses of Parliament, London

Olaudah Equiano

Abolitionist

Olaudah Equiano was born in 1745 in the Eboe province (southern Nigeria). At around the age of 11, he was kidnapped with his sister, sold by local slave traders, and shipped across the Atlantic to Barbados and then Virginia, USA.

In Virginia he was sold to Lieutenant Michael Pascal, a Royal Navy officer, who renamed him Gustavus Vassa after the 16th-century Swedish king. For eight years, Equiano travelled the oceans with Pascal, during which time he was baptised and learned to read and write.

Equiano was sold to a ship captain in London who took him to Montserrat and resold him to Robert King, a prominent merchant. While working as a deckhand, valet and barber for King, Equiano earned money by trading on the side. Only three years later, he had enough money to buy his freedom.

For the next twenty years, Equiano travelled the world, visiting places including the Arctic and Turkey. In 1786, he became involved in the movement to abolish slavery and a prominent member of the 'Sons of Africa', a group of 12 black men campaigning for abolition.

In 1789, Equiano published his autobiography, *'The Interesting Narrative of the Life of Olaudah Equiano or Gustavus Vassa, the African'*, one of the earliest books published by a black writer. The book became popular and helped the abolitionist cause. In 1792, Equiano married Susanna Cullen and they had two daughters. Equiano died in 1797, aged 52.

Sislin Fay Allen

Britain's First Black Policewoman

Sislin Fay Allen joined the Metropolitan Police in 1968, becoming the first black WPC.

Sislin Fay Allen saw an advert appealing for male and female police officers while flicking through a newspaper. At the time, there were no black female officers so the mum-of-two sat down and wrote an application. Within a few weeks, Sislin had made it to the interview stage and was accepted into the force.

The first prejudices Sislin experienced came from her own community for joining the police force. The perception of the police was poor and the role was considered degrading. After her training and passing out ceremony Sislin was stationed in Croydon so she could be close to her family. She later transferred to Scotland Yard and then Norbury police station.

Sislin's appointment as the Metropolitan Police's first black female police officer prompted some hate mail, which she was never shown.

In 1972, Sislin left the Metropolitan Police and returned to her husband's birth country of Jamaica with their children. She joined the Jamaican police force before later returning to the UK with her family and settling in South London.

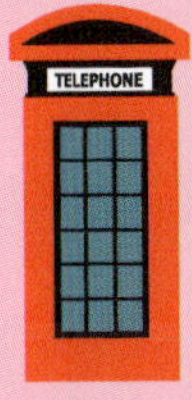

John Anthony Roberts

First Black QC at Queen's Counsel

John Anthony Roberts was the first lawyer of African ancestry to be a QC at Queen's Counsel, the highest ranking for barristers. He was also the first black lawyer to be the head of his chambers, to be made a Recorder of the Crown Court, and to be appointed by the British government to a dependent territory as a High Court Judge of the Supreme Courts of the British Virgin Islands & Anguilla, British West Indies. John was also the first Head of Chambers to accept seven female barristers as tenants in 1975, a record during that era.

John worked as a civil servant in the UK between 1964 – 1969. In 1966, driven by the desire to help people, he started to read law part-time at the Inns of Court School of Law.

John was called to the bar (Gray's Inn) in 1969, becoming a Master in 1996, and helped set up a chambers at 9 Stone Buildings, Lincoln's Inn, in 1970. Later, In 1975, he set up his own chambers at 2 Stone Buildings, ensuring that his set of chambers was fully representative, mixed and diverse with Asian, white, black African and Caribbean members.

John took silk in 1988 and was the first person of African origin to do so and later became a High Court Judge in the British Virgin Islands & Anguilla, both British West Indies Dependent Territories.

John was called to the bars of 10 other countries: Jamaica (1973), Sierra Leone (1975), Trinidad & Tobago (1978), Bahamas (1984), St Kitts & Nevis (1988), Antigua (2002), Barbados (2002), Bermuda (2003), Anguilla (2006) and Grenada (2007).

John was known as a modest and humble man, continuing to serve following his retirement as President of the British West Indian Ex-Servicemen and Ex-Servicewomen's Association, as well as serving as joint President of the British Caribbean Association.

Dame Linda Dobbs DBE

Britain's First Black Judge

Dame Linda Penelope Dobbs, DBE, a retired High Court judge in England and Wales, served from 2004 to 2013. Dobbs was the first non-white person to be appointed to the senior judiciary of England and Wales.

In 2004, following a successful career at the bar, Dame Linda became the first non-white high court judge in the UK.

At the bar she was a member of a number of committees, including the Race Relations, Equal Opportunities, International, Professional Conduct and Professional Standard Committees. She became the Chairman of the Criminal Bar Association in 2003, setting up its first Equality and Diversity sub-committee.

During her time on the High Court Bench, Dame Linda was the Chair of the Magisterial Committee of the Judicial Studies Board, Senior Liaison Judge for Diversity, and Chair of the International Committee of the Judicial College and a Fawcett Commissioner.

Did you know?

On 'Red Letter Days', such as the Queen's birthday, high court judges wear a scarlet robe.

Dame Linda has been involved in the training of lawyers and judges both in the UK and internationally for over 20 years and is a contributing editor to a number of legal training publications. She is the Director of Training at the Judicial Institute for Africa, based at the University of Cape Town, where she is an honorary professor. She is a patron of a number of charities (including two in Sierra Leone and two in South Africa) and sits on a number of advisory committees. She is the immediate past President of ILFA (International Lawyers for Africa) and chair of the UK-Sierra Leone Pro Bono Network. Dame Linda is a patron of the African Prisons Project and an initiator of the 18 Red Lion Court Award for African advocates. She is also patron of Masicorp, an NGO promoting education in Masiphumelele, South Africa.

Dame Linda has been named as one of Britain's most powerful black women and one of the 100 Great Black Britons, featuring regularly in the Power List 100 of Influential Black Britons.

Sally S J Penni MBE

Barrister and Champion of Diversity in the Workplace

Sally SJ Penni MBE is a barrister at law and practising lawyer in Manchester and London. Sally Penni is a Master of the Benches of Gray's Inn, a governor role, and one of the youngest black women to be so elected.

Sally was called to the bar in 2000 by the Honourable Society of Gray's Inn, London.

She is the first black female barrister on the northern circuit to be honoured in the Queen's birthday honours list in 2020 with an MBE, along with footballer and food poverty campaigner Marcus Rashford, the Manchester United footballer, and Brian Cox, CBE, a physicist and former keyboard player with D:Ream.

Sally SJ Penni MBE

Queen Elizabeth II

Sally Penni works in Criminal Law and Employment Law, specialising in vulnerable witnesses and young offenders with protected characteristics. She is married with three children. She is an author and podcast host of Talking Law with over 60,000 listeners. Penni is the founder of Women in the Law UK.

Sally Penni specialises in vulnerable witnesses and young offenders with protected characteristics

Rochdale Millworkers

Abolition Supporters

The cotton industry that served the factories of Britain's industrial revolution came from the southern states in America.

African slaves were used to pick cotton, and after slavery was made illegal in the British Empire in 1833, a blockade was established. However, this was broken by millowners except for one mill in Rochdale. They supported the abolition of slavery during the American Civil War.

Cotton mill in Lancashire

By ceasing to support the cotton slave trade, there was a massive shortage of cotton for the mills of Lancashire and this huge industry, which had grown enormously and supported many families, was brought to a stand-still.

Even though there followed a cotton famine in 1862-3, the Rochdale protestors continued their support against slavery and would no longer work with cotton that had been picked by slaves.

Slaves leaving a cotton plantation

The US President, Abraham Lincoln, acknowledged what the people of Rochdale had done, and sent ships packed with food and supplies to Lancashire from the US. Today there is a blue plaque commemorating the Millworkers of Rochdale, and a statue of President Lincoln in Lincoln Square, Manchester.

Did you know?

Cotton grows on a plant. It is collected into bales, before being spun into yarn, which is then woven into fabrics we can use for clothing, bedding, bags, toys and many other things!

Cotton field

I. Stephanie Boyce

President of The Law Society in England and Wales

In October 2021, I. Stephanie Boyce became the 177th President, the sixth female and the first non-white person to hold the post in the history of the Law Society of England and Wales.

I. Stephanie's Story

"I began my life journey in Aylesbury, Buckinghamshire a place where I would come back to time and time again. Aylesbury in the 1970s when I was growing up there was a small country, sleepy market town with little ethnic diversity compared to today's diverse large ancient market town.

"I grew up with the sounds of injustices ringing in my ears. Domestically and globally I could see people struggling to exercise their rights and this is what inspired me to join the legal profession. To become a solicitor.

"After living in Aylesbury for a number of years, at the age of 12 I went to live in America with my mother. America would have a lasting impression upon me. I was overwhelmed by the poverty, the injustices, and the people unable to access justice because of their low socio-economic position. There were people struggling to exercise their rights, people having little or no rights because of the colour of their skin; oh how I longed to make a difference, to have my voice heard. To encourage and inspire the voiceless to speak.

"In 1991, I returned to the UK to live and study, but not before I came across my first barrier. My US qualification, my high school diploma was not enough to allow me entry to a British university. I would spend another two years undertaking an access to higher qualification diploma. This enabled me to enter London Guildhall University as it was then named in February 1996 as a part time student, whilst working part time at British Rail. By September of that year I had enrolled full time leaving behind my life in Aylesbury and all things familiar, packing up my worldly goods in my car and heading to Mile End. How I longed for home, the familiarity of that old market town, the parish church of St Mary, the canal, the views of the town and beyond.

"In June 1999 I graduated with a LLB(Hons) with politics. In September 1999 I entered the College of Law, Guildford where I would study and complete the Legal Practice Course (LPC), the final academic qualification on my route to becoming

a solicitor. In 2000, the year of the Millennium Bug I commenced my training contract, the last hurdle to becoming a qualified solicitor. Again, I would return to Aylesbury, the "spiritual cradle of the Paralympics", the place where my dream had started all those years ago as a young child. I would commence my training contract, my two-year training period in the historic part of Aylesbury, Temple Street, with a local firm, a stone's throw from Bucks County Museum in Church Street.

"Having walked into the firm for the first time as a trainee solicitor in 2000, I would walk out for the final time as a qualified solicitor in 2002, an officer of the court, with an overriding duty to the rule of law and the administration of justice.

"The legal profession in general, and solicitors specifically, have a clear role to play in championing the values and concepts of justice, fairness, equity, and legitimacy and never more so than now. I'm often reminding myself to not lose my joy in the difficulties of life. I write this in the middle of a pandemic called Covid 19; which has claimed the lives worldwide of over 780,000 people, no country, no place has been left untouched. The virus is a stark reminder that life is precious and for living. Many dreams have been placed on hold whilst we wait for the virus to pass and a vaccine to be found. If but not for the pandemic I would now be the Vice President of the Law Society, instead I remain the deputy Vice President, a delay of three months to allow colleagues and I the opportunity to deal with the impact of the pandemic on the profession.

"In October 2021 I will become the 177th, the sixth female and the first non-white person to hold the post in the history of the Law Society of England and Wales. I am determined to leave the legal profession more diverse and inclusive than the one I entered. That more must be done to remove barriers, open doors and confront unacceptable behaviours that do not allow everyone the opportunity to succeed and make the most of their talents regardless of their race, gender, disability, sexuality, religion or background.

"My story is one of resilience and determination, a burning desire to stand by my dream until it was realised, a definite purpose and one I was prepared to stand by until it was achieved. "Four times", it took me four times before I was successfully elected as deputy Vice President. I was not prepared to quit because of temporary setbacks.

"If you have ever been discouraged, faced difficulties that have taken the very soul out of you, marooned you in the desert of despair, been knocked back, faced hurdles, that no matter where you are in life, you too can reach your full potential if you are willing to get into action. To train your mind towards your definite purpose. To never quit."

(Bucks County Museum, 2020)

Did you know?

1. Stephanie Boyce became the first black president of England and Wales in 2021. The Law Society is the professional body for all solicitors.

You can read the original article here:
www.buckscountymuseum.org/museum/stephanies-story-black-history-month

Mary Seacole

The Black Florence Nightingale

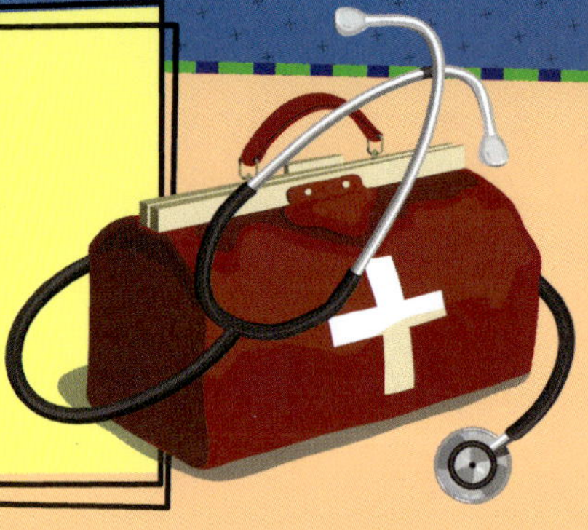

Mary Seacole was born in Kingston, Jamaica, in 1805, to her Jamaican mother and Scottish father. Mary learned her nursing skills from her mother who kept a boarding house for wounded soldiers. Despite being of dual heritage, Mary and her family had few civil rights. They couldn't vote or enter many professions.

In 1854, after travelling to England, Mary approached the War Office, asking to be sent to the Crimea as a war nurse. The War Office refused. Undeterred, Mary funded her own trip and established the British Hotel for sick and convalescent soldiers, often risking her life on the frontline to tend to the dying and wounded.

Mary Seacole

After the war, Mary returned to England and became destitute and unwell. After the press highlighted her plight, a benefit festival was organised in Kennington, south London, in July 1857 to raise money for her. The fundraiser is believed to have attracted thousands of people. Later that year, Seacole published her memoirs, *The Wonderful Adventures of Mrs Seacole in Many Lands*.

Mary Seacole died on 14 May 1881.

A statue of Seacole was erected opposite the Houses of Parliament in the grounds of St Thomas' hospital in 2016.

William Cuffay

Chartist Leader in Early Victorian London

Born on a merchant ship in the West Indies in 1788, William Cuffay was the son of a naval cook and former enslaved person from St Kitts. The family eventually settled in Chatham, Kent, after William trained as a tailor.

In Victorian times, you couldn't buy clothes from shops like we do. You had to make them yourself, or pay a tailor to do it!

Cuffay played a leading role in the Chartist movement and was elected to the national executive of the National Charter Association in 1842. In August 1848, Cuffay was arrested for conspiring to levy war against the Queen. He was sentenced to transportation to Tasmania, where he returned to work as a tailor.

Find Out!

Britain's governments were made up of wealthy landowners, who were not democratically voted in. The Chartist Movement created *The People's Charter*, they wanted to create an equal political and voting system. Can you think why this would be important?

Chartist leaders were arrested across England after many riots broke out

Claudia Jones

Founder of the Notting Hill Carnival

Born in Belmont, Port-of-Spain, Trinidad, in 1915, Claudia Jones lived much of her life in New York before she was deported from the US for being an active member of the US Communist party. She was given asylum in England in 1955. In England, Claudia threw herself into anti-racist activism and is considered the founder of the Notting Hill Carnival.

In response to the Notting Hill riots of 1958 and the racist murder of Kelso Cochrane, Jones launched an indoor Caribbean carnival in St Pancras in 1959 with the intention of bringing people together. Further indoor events were held throughout the 1960s, finally taking to the streets of Notting Hill, West London, in 1965.

Notting Hill Carnival takes place over two days every year in August. There is music, performance, and celebration.

How Many?

Approximately how many people attend the Notting Hill Carnival each year?

Samuel Coleridge-Taylor

Black Classical Composer

Samuel Coleridge-Taylor was born in Holborn, London, on 15 August 1875 and raised in Croydon. He was one of few black classical composers to catch the imagination of the white British musical establishment, coming to prominence in 1898 at the Gloucester Festival with an orchestral Ballade in A Minor, followed by his much acclaimed trilogy Hiawatha's Wedding Feast (1898).

Find and Listen!

Can you name five black British classical musicians from the 20th Century? Try listening to some of their music. Which do you like best?

Coleridge-Taylor died aged 37 after he collapsed at West Croydon station while waiting for a train. His funeral procession through Croydon was lined for three and a half miles by crowds with their heads bared.

Olive Morris

Youth Member of the Black Panther Movement

Born in Jamaica in 1952, Olive Morris moved to south London as a young child with her siblings to be with her parents.

Olive was just 17 when she became a leading figure in Britain's anti-racism movement in the 1960s and 70s. She took action against discrimination in housing and employment, attacks by far-right groups such as the National Front, and stop and search of black people. Morris was a member of the youth section of the Black Panther movement in the UK.

Find out!

Can you learn more about the purpose of the Olive Morris Memorial Awards? Do you know of someone who could be nominated for this award?

Olive became ill while on holiday in Spain and was diagnosed with non-Hodgkin's lymphoma, a form of cancer, upon her return home. She died on 12 July 1979 aged 27 at St Thomas' hospital in London.

Did you know?

Despite her short life, Olive Morris was a leading political activist and helped build the Black Women's Movement in the UK.

Jack Leslie

Professional Footballer

Jack Leslie was a successful footballer. He was the only black professional player in England during his time with Plymouth Argyle and was expected to become England's first black player, however, he was denied the opportunity when selectors became aware of his heritage.

Jack joined Plymouth Argyle in 1921 and after 14 seasons (primarily as a centre-forward) he scored 133 league goals in 384 games which makes him the club's fourth highest goal-scorer. In 2019, the club named a stand in Jack's honour.

In 1925, Jack was called up to play for the national squad for England v Ireland, however he was removed at the last minute. Apparently, there were objections to his colour. Jack was never picked to play for England again. He retired from football in 1935.

Find Out!

Who was the first black player to play for England and in what year?

Did you know?

In the 1920s footballs and football boots were brown and made of leather! The boots would have been much heavier to wear, and the balls were much heavier to kick!

Recently there has been a campaign by the football fans of Plymouth Argyle to get a statue of Jack Leslie commissioned.

After running a successful crowdfunding campaign a sculpture was comissioned to create a statue of Jack Leslie in 2021.

Ottobah Cugoano

Abolitionist

Born in 1757 near Ajumako, Ghana, Ottobah Cugoano, also known as John Stuart, was an abolitionist, political activist and natural rights philosopher.

Slaves working on a sugar plantation

Aged 13, Ottobah was sold into slavery and shipped to Grenada where he worked on an island plantation. In 1772, he was bought by an English merchant who baptised him as John Stuart. He learnt to read and write and was later freed, joining the 'Sons of Africa' abolition group.

Cugoano worked as a servant for artists Richard and Maria Cosway

In 1787, he published *Thoughts and Sentiments on the Evil and Wicked Traffic of the Slavery and Commerce of the Human Species*. Despite being one of the first pieces of writing by a black Briton about slavery, the book consists mostly of religious and philosophical argument rather than Cugoano's own experiences.

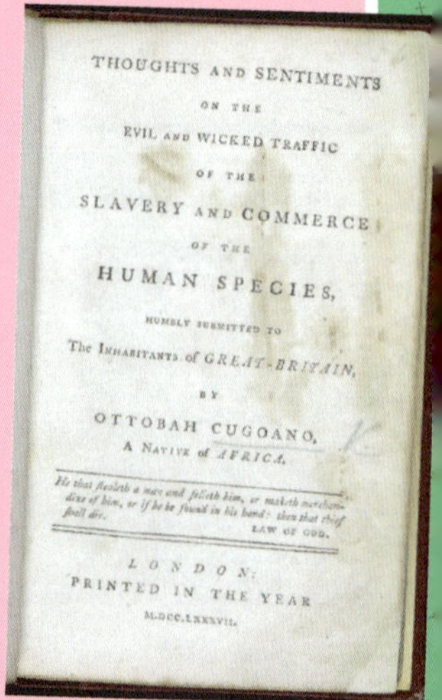

THOUGHTS AND SENTIMENTS
ON THE
EVIL AND WICKED TRAFFIC
OF THE
SLAVERY AND COMMERCE
OF THE
HUMAN SPECIES,
HUMBLY SUBMITTED TO
The INHABITANTS of GREAT-BRITAIN,
BY
OTTOBAH CUGOANO,
A NATIVE of AFRICA.

He that stealeth a man and selleth him, or maketh merchandize of him, or if he be found in his hand: then that thief shall die.
LAW OF GOD.

LONDON:
PRINTED IN THE YEAR
M.DCC.LXXXVII.

Cugoano travelled around Britain promoting his book, contributing his voice and first-hand personal testimony to the campaign against the slave trade. He died in 1791.

Walter Tull

Professional Footballer and Soldier

886,000 soldiers died during the First World War.

Walter Tull played for Tottenham Hotspur Football Club. He was one of the first black professional football players in England, later playing for Northampton Town while overcoming racial discrimination. He also become one of the most celebrated black British soldiers of the war, leading men into battle during the First World War at a time when the army opposed a person of non-European descent becoming an officer.

Walter died aged 29 while leading an attack during the second Battle of the Somme. Private Thomas Billingham, a fellow footballer, saw him killed and tried to retrieve his body so he could have a proper burial. However, Tull's body was never recovered.

Tull is remembered on the memorial wall in the Faubourg d'Amiens cemetery in Arras, along with 35,000 soldiers whose bodies were never recovered from the battlefields. Research by Andy Robertshaw, a military historian, suggests that Tull may have been buried in unmarked graves at Heninel-Croisilles Road cemetery in northern France. A statue commemorating Walter Tull resides in Northampton.

Did you know?

West Indian soldiers and black Britons served in the army and navy during the First World War. The contributions of the 15,204 men who served in the British West Indies Regiment have largely been forgotten in the UK's remembrance of the great war.

Statue of Walter Tull in Northampton England

Ena Collymore-Woodstock

WWII Veteran

Ena Collymore-Woodstock was one of the first women to set sail from the Caribbean to help the allied forces in response to a recruitment advert.

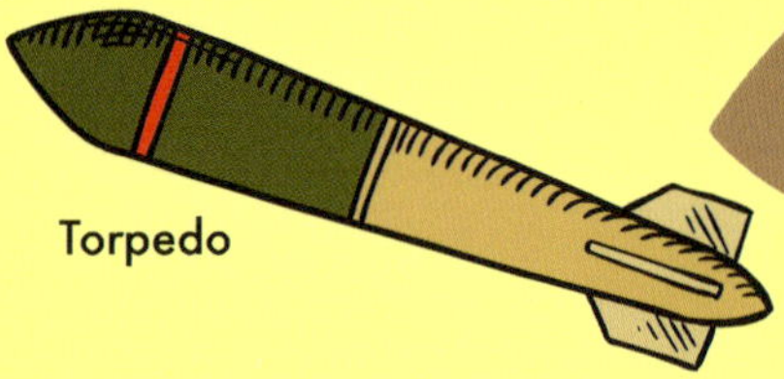

Torpedo

Did you know?

Ena served in the Auxiliary Territorial Service (ATS), which was the first branch of the British Army for women only. Queen Elizabeth II was also a member from 1945.

Ena arrived in London having survived a torpedo strike on the boat she travelled on, facing racism and sexism while in the UK. Ena became the first black woman radar operator defending UK's coast after refusing a clerical job at the War Office.

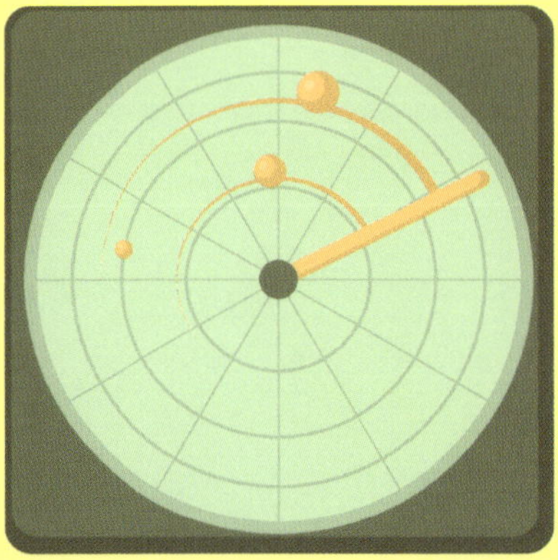

Radar Screen

After leaving the military in 1946, Ena was the first woman of colour to train at Gray's Inn and after being called to the Bar in England in 1948, she returned to Jamaica to serve as the clerk of courts for St James' Parish.

By 1959 Ena had made history by becoming the first female resident magistrate in Jamaica.

In 2020 at age 103, Ena is believed to be the oldest surviving WWII female veteran.

UK coastline

The Windrush Generation

The Empire Windrush carried 493 passengers on its voyage from Jamaica to the UK. The journey took 30 days.

After the Second World War, the UK invited those from colonies to come to England to help rebuild the country. Due to a shortage of workers, thousands of men and women came to Britain from the Caribbean to work in sectors including manufacturing, public transport and the NHS.

In June 1948, the Empire Windrush arrived at Tilbury Docks, Essex, carrying hundreds of people from the Caribbean on the promise of citizenship and right of abode in the UK as members of the British Empire when they arrived. They were not welcomed with open arms, and neither was citizenship granted. The people lived in cramped conditions and endured racist and unkind remarks. These people became known as the Windrush generation.

Some of the black people you see in England today were born here, and their parents and grandparents were from the Windrush generation. In 2018, people from this generation were wrongly detained, denied legal rights, threatened with deportation, and, in at least 83 cases, wrongly deported from the UK by the Home Office.

The Windrush generation were pivotal in helping us to rebuild our country post World War II so we must always be grateful to them and celebrate them in British black history.

Cheddar Man

The First Modern Briton

The first modern Briton, thought to have lived around 300 generations ago, had black skin, blue eyes and dark, curly hair. Known as Cheddar Man, Britain's oldest complete skeleton was unearthed more than a century ago in Gough's Cave, Somerset.

DNA analysis revealed that Cheddar Man likely died in his twenties and had a relatively good diet. He lived in Britain when it was almost completely depopulated. Previous populations were wiped out before him – Cheddar Man marked the start of continuous habitation on the island.

Genetically, Cheddar Man belonged to a group of people known as the "western hunter-gatherers". His ancestors migrated to Europe from the Middle East after the Ice Age. Today, it is thought that 10 per cent of white British people are descended from this group.

Research!

What else can you find out about 'Cheddar Man'?

Britain's oldest complete skeleton was dicovered in a cave in Somerset!

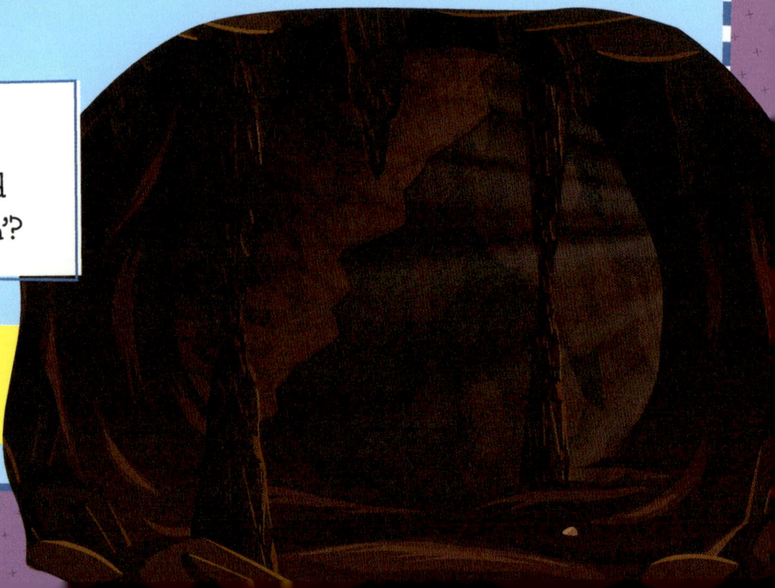

Eric Irons OBE

The First Black Magistrate

Eric was born in Jamaica and recruited into the RAF in 1944. He eventually settled in Nottingham. His passion for racial equality led him into public life.

During the 1950s, Eric campaigned for better employment opportunities, health and education for black workers. As a result of his campaign, black employment increased. Eric was subsequently awarded an OBE in 1977.

Find out!

People who have done very special things in Britain are sometimes awarded an OBE or MBE. Can you list other people from this book who have been awarded an OBE or MBE?

Did you know?

There is a commemorative black plaque at the National Justice Museum in Nottingham, in memory of Eric Irons' work as Britain's first black magistrate.

What is a magistrate?

Anyone can be a magistrate. They are Justices of the Peace and volunteer judges who sit on criminal and family cases. They are not paid but can claim expenses.

Magistrates can send people to prison for up to six months and they can take people's children away from them.

It's important to have diverse people making decisions about people's lives. These need to be all ages, all backgrounds, and all races, genders, sexuality and communities.

Sir Arthur Lewis

The First Black Professor

Sir William Arthur Lewis (23 January 1915 – 15 June 1991) was a Saint Lucian economist and the James Madison Professor of Political Economy at Princeton University. He was well known for his contributions in the field of economic development and was awarded the Nobel Memorial Prize in Economic Sciences in 1979.

He was a professor at the University of Manchester when he was 33. He published his first book on economics in 1949 and continued to write about how labour, class and commodities affected the world's economy.

Did you know?

Sir Arthur Lewis established the Caribbean Development Bank between 1970-1973 which invested in Caribbean countries.

And he was even a Google Doodle in December 2020!

Discover!

Sir Arthur Lewis published several books on the study of economics. Can you find out how many he wrote, and what 'the study of economics' means?

Paul Leroy Robeson

Actor, Singer and Activist

Paul Robeson (April 9, 1898 – January 23, 1976) was an American bass baritone concert artist and stage and film actor. He became famous for his cultural accomplishments and for his political activism.

Paul's political activities began with his involvement with unemployed workers and anti-imperialist students whom he met in Britain. In the United States he became active in the Civil Rights Movement and other social justice campaigns.

Paul Robeson performed in many stage shows in Britain, settling in London for several years with his wife Eslanda. During this period, Robeson became increasingly attuned to the sufferings of people of other cultures, notably the British working class and the colonised people of the British Empire.

Did you know?

As well as being a singer and actor, Robeson had excelled at sports when he was at college!

Listen or Watch!

Ask a grown-up to help you find a clip of Paul Robeson singing a famous song called *Ol' Man River* from a movie called Showboat, from 1936.

Scene from Othello with Paul Robeson as Othello and Uta Hagen as Desdemona, Theatre Guild Production, Broadway, 1943-44

Marcus Rashford MBE

Professional Footballer

Marcus Rashford MBE – professional footballer who plays for the England national team and premier league club Manchester United.

In 2020, Marcus collaborated with the food waste charity, FairShare, to help children in Greater Manchester who were no longer receiving school meals. The initiative raised over £20 million and helped children across the whole of the UK, providing four million meals in one month alone.

He continued and successfully campaigned to combat child hunger by petitioning the UK government to provide economically disadvantaged children with free school meals during school holidays, not just term time. This change in policy helped over a million children.

He has also teamed up with chefs to help create recipes and online videos to promote healthy and affordable ways to combat child hunger.

As well as winning a Pride of Britain Award in 2020, he was also awarded an MBE as acknowledgement of his contribution and efforts.

Did you know?

Marcus Rashford was only seven years old when he joined Manchester United's youth academy!

Have a try!

Why don't you try asking a grown up to help you make a yummy, healthy meal to eat with your friends or family?

Can love conquer hate?

In 2021 the UEFA Euro football tournament was played, after being postponed from 2020 due to the Covid-19 pandemic.

Before every game, the players (black and white) took the knee as a sign of protest that Black Lives Matter too.

The England football team did not lose a game and for over a month they brought the nation joy. After 55 years, England got to the final of a major championship, facing Italy.

The team represented all that was good about Britain. Black players included Raheem Sterling, Marcus Rashford, Jadon Sancho and Bukayo Saka. After the match ended with a 1-1 draw, the championship was decided in a shoot-out with Italy winning 3-2.

After weeks of exhilarating football and a nation energised by optimism, the hard-fought game ended in devastation – not only for the England team but especially the three players who missed their penalty shots.

Sancho, Saka and Rashford all received racist abuse both online and off, marring what had been a courageous and patriotic sporting event for England, and indeed the United Kingdom.

After the Euro final, hooligans wrote racial abuse on a mural of Marcus painted by artist Akse in Manchester in tribute to his work on child food poverty. The response from football fans and local residents was to cover the graffiti with messages of support, solidarity and love.

Despite the loss and the subsequent abhorrent racial abuse, much of the country and football fans around the world rose to the players' defence and excitement remains high for England in the World Cup in 2022.

Take a look!

You can explore the messages left on the Marcus Rashford mural by visiting the digital 'Wall of Hope'.
bthopeunited.com/wallofhope

"Darkness cannot drive out darkness; only light can do that.
Hate cannot drive out hate; only love can do that."

Martin Luther King Jr

Some Role Models From Outside the UK

The following people aren't British, however, they have inspired so many British people from afar.

Nelson Mandela

(18 July 1918 – 5 December 2013)

Born in 1918, Nelson Mandela was a South African lawyer, anti-apartheid revolutionary, political leader and philanthropist who served as President of South Africa from 1994 to 1999. He was the country's first black head of state and the first elected in a fully representative democratic election.

Nelson Mandela's political work made him a target for the apartheid regime. When the African National Congress was banned in 1960, he became the leader of Umkhonto we Sizwe (MK), the armed wing of the Congress. In 1962, he was sentenced to five years in prison for instigating a strike and leaving the country illegally. In 1963, Nelson joined other MK leaders in the Rivonia Trial, at the end of which he was sentenced to life in prison for sabotage and attempting to overthrow the South African government.

Nelson Mandela was finally released from prison in 1990 after over 27 years of unbroken incarceration.

Rosa Parks

(4 February 1913 – 24 October 2005)

Rosa Parks was an American activist in the civil rights movement. Racial segregation was normal, with buses having separate white-only and 'coloured' sections. However, Rosa Parks changed that. On December 1, 1955, in Montgomery, Alabama, Rosa refused to give up her seat to a white passenger in the 'coloured' section after the whites-only section was filled.

Rosa's standing in the community and her willingness to become a controversial figure inspired the black community to boycott the Montgomery buses for over a year. This was the first major campaign of the post-war civil rights movement. In November 1956, the courts decided that bus segregation was unconstitutional under the Equal Protection Clause of the 14th Amendment to the U.S. Constitution.

Rosa became an international icon of resistance to racial segregation, organising and collaborating with civil rights leaders including Martin Luther King Jr. Although

widely honoured in later years for her act of defiance, Rosa also suffered. She was fired from her job, and received death threats many years afterwards.

In her final years, Rosa suffered from dementia. She received a number of medals, including the Presidential Medal of Freedom, and a posthumous statue in the United States Capitol's National Statuary Hall. After her death in 2005, Rosa was the first woman to lie in the Capitol Rotunda, becoming the thirty-first person to receive this honour.

Rosa Parks Day is commemorated on February 4th, her birthday, in California and Missouri while Ohio and Oregon commemorate the occasion on December 1st, the anniversary of the day she was arrested.

Martin Luther King

(15 January 1929 – 4 April 1968)

Martin Luther King Jr. was an American Christian minister and activist. He became the most visible spokesperson and leader in the civil rights movement from 1955 until his assassination in 1968. Inspired by his Christian beliefs and the nonviolent activism of Mahatma Gandhi, King advanced civil rights through nonviolence and civil disobedience.

King led the 1955 Montgomery bus boycott and later became the first president of the Southern Christian Leadership Conference (SCLC), leading struggles against segregation and helping to organise non-violent protests. In 1963, King delivered his famous "I Have a Dream" speech on the steps of the Lincoln Memorial.

On October 14, 1964, King won the Nobel Peace Prize for combating racial inequality through nonviolent resistance. In his final years, he expanded his focus towards poverty, capitalism, and the Vietnam War.

King was assassinated on April 4th in Memphis, Tennessee, triggering riots in many U.S. cities. He was posthumously awarded the Presidential Medal of Freedom and the Congressional Gold Medal.

Martin Luther King Jr. Day was established as a holiday in cities and states throughout the United States beginning in 1971. Hundreds of streets in the U.S. have been renamed in his honour.

Josephine Baker

(3 June 1906 – 12 April 1975)

Josephine Baker was an American-born French entertainer, French Resistance agent, and civil rights activist. She was the first black woman to star in a major motion picture, the 1927 silent film Siren of the Tropics.

Josephine refused to perform for segregated audiences in the United States and is noted for her contributions to the civil rights movement. She was celebrated by artists of the era, who dubbed her the "Black Venus", the "Black Pearl", the "Bronze Venus", and the "Creole Goddess". She aided the French Resistance during World War II.

Josephine was awarded the Croix de guerre by the French military, and was named a Chevalier of the Légion d'honneur by General Charles de Gaulle.

Harriet Tubman

(1822 – 1913)

Born Araminta Ross, Harriet Tubman was an abolitionist and political activist. Born into slavery, Harriet escaped and made 13 missions to rescue roughly 70 enslaved people, including friends and family. Her missions were aided by the Underground Railroad – a network of antislavery activists and safe houses.

First job at 5?

Harriet was sent to her first job when she was just 5 or 6! She looked after the baby of a wealthy family. Could you care for a baby when you were 5?

This statue of Harriet Tubman is situated in Harlem, New York

Harriet Tubman

Kamala Harris

First Black Vice President of USA

Joe Biden

Kamala Harris

Kamala Harris is a significant international figure. Kamala Harris became the first black Vice President of the USA to President Joe Biden in the 2020 election.

The White House, Washington DC

Kamala's heritage is Indian and Jamaican. She was born in the USA. Prior to becoming VP of the USA, she was a lawyer and prosecutor. This position means a lot to women and black minorities everywhere, not just in the USA. The Biden and Harris presidency succeeded the Donald J Trump and Mike Pence presidency.

Kamala Harris appointment as VP means a lot to women and black minorities everywhere

Did you know?

The first black President of the USA was Barack Obama. He was President for 8 years from January 2009 to 2017.

Conclusion

I am a lawyer and I love history. I enjoy going to museums and galleries and often wonder where all the black and brown people are. What was their contribution to black history? I don't want to travel all the way to Liverpool to find out about slavery, or to Bristol or Falmouth in Cornwall. I would like to be able to read about it as part of everyday life which is what inspired me to write this book. Britain is a small island with an incredibly rich and diverse history. Let this unite us not divide us.

Because black history is all our history.

I did not include the sports stars and the TV stars and the obvious celebrities that older readers may be familiar with. For example, Trevor McDonald and Moira Stewart whom I grew up with, reading the news on TV, or Joan Armatrading whose music I love. Instead, I deliberately chose lesser known characters who played a forgotten yet pivotal role in our history.

I hope you found this book as interesting as I did in writing about some of these brilliant figures from history. Of course, it is not all the history, just a brief yet significant snapshot in time. But I hope that, going forward, we can all celebrate black history together, and that you continue your exploration into our lesser known past. It is my hope that Black History Month will soon become part of our general knowledge and a truer and more accurate reflection of history will be taught as part of the schools' curriculum.

If you are a teacher, please use this book as a learning resource. I have also included a list of recommended books to aid learning in your school and in your work place.

I am grateful to my children for encouraging me to write this book. I am also grateful to the brilliant teachers at my children's school who said there was an appetite for the book. I am especially grateful for the leadership of Mr How the headteacher who understands the importance of diversity and community. Thank you to Mrs Hardy, Mrs Silva, Mrs Noden, Ms Ulett and all of the team who recognise the importance of black history. And thank you to Mr Dan Berry for reminding me of the X-Men and Marvel comics.

I hope that you will send me some of the hidden figures from black British history that you have discovered for me to write about in future editions of this book.

Further Reading

Little Leaders: Bold Women in Black History by Vashti Harrison

Young, Gifted and Black by Jamia Wilson

Black and British: A Forgotten History by David Olusoga

Black and British: A Short, Essential History (for young readers) by David Olusoga

100 Great Black Britons by Patrick Vernon and Angelina Osbourne

Activities

You can do some of these activities during Black History Month at school or at home.

- Choose one figure from history and find out more information about them.
- Can you make a PowerPoint presentation of one of the characters from the book?
- Can you find a famous figure NOT in this book?
- What is your heritage? Might you be related to the 'Beachy Head Woman', for example?
- Can you think of some books you could write and an era in history you could find out about?
- What type of food do they eat in the Caribbean where the Windrush generation came from?
- What type of food did they eat in the world wars? Can you find out?
- What clues does archaeology teach us about history and black history?
- What area of history would you like to learn about next?
- If you could build a time machine, what part of history would you like to go back to and why?

Share your answers and activities with *@sallypenni1* using hashtag *#blackhistoryisallourhistory*

About The Author

Sally Penni is married with 3 children and lives in Manchester. She is an award-winning Barrister at Law. In 2020, Sally was awarded an MBE for services to diversity in the workplace, social mobility and to the Law. Outside of the courtroom, Sally hosts and produces a podcast called Talking Law with Sally Penni MBE, with over 80,000 listeners and includes interviews with actress Maxine Peake and Judge Rinder. Sally has also authored a number of legal and professional development books and has a great love of history.

Sally is a proponent of black history and champions diversity in the workplace. During Black History Month in October 2020, she began to research some of Britain's black history and found some interesting stories to share.

In addition to ***Where Are You From?*** Sally Penni (SJ Penni) is an author of various children's and business books. She can be contacted to speak at Festivals and Events.

The ***Talking Law*** book series includes episodes from her podcasts, and Sally also publishes professional and career development books.

Sally co-authors the ***Rosie and the Unicorn*** children's book series with her daughter Maddie S-J.

For more information on the author:

www.sallypenniauthor.co.uk

@sallypenni1
@sjsallypenni
linkedin.com/in/sallypenni
talkinglaw.libsyn.com

Half of the proceeds from sales of this book will help these charities:

The Black Curriculum – set up and run by CEO Lavinya Stennett

ACLT – a charity that helps children find bone marrow donors from black and minority communities

Acknowledgements

First of all, it's hard work being a lawyer and a mother, so writing another book means there are people to thank. I have many people to thank for the support which has made it possible.

Firstly, there would not even be a book without my lovely children, who have been patient with my research and ideas for a book about black history. They are thrilled to have something to read in Black History Month and have conversation starters.

Secondly, my husband who is patient with all of my projects and forever asking why I am writing in the first place. Admittedly, this is said by him when I am writing legal documents! But he is astonished once he sees my books come to life covering important issues.

The black and white illustrations in the book and on the cover are by my brother Julian Penni, a talented artist, an architect by trade and a brilliant father of three. Even though he is very busy, he still found some time to draw the hidden figures from history.

Thank you, Team Author UK. Especially Sarah Fountain, for her design.

During the completion of this book, the delayed Euro 2020 football championship played in 2021 during the Covid-19 pandemic. England made history by reaching the finals. However, due to missed penalties from three black players, they received racist abuse through social media and Marcus Rashford's mural in Withington, Manchester, was defaced. The nation's response was to condemn such abuse and prove that love, not hate, conquers racism. The incident proved that we still need to have conversations about race and racism in the UK and globally. I want to thank the people of Manchester for their support of me and my work, inside and outside the courtroom. I also wish to extend my thanks to Marcus Rashford for all he does for child poverty. He was awarded his MBE in the same honours list as myself by her Majesty the Queen.

Finally, a massive, heartfelt thank you to you, my lovely readers. If you did not read my books, there would be no point in writing them for the children and, of course, all the grown-ups.